THE BROKEN BYPASS

BRUCE MARTIN

THE BROKEN BYPASS BY BRUCE MARTIN

A young African emerging writer with raw unapologetic truth bombs as weapons.
And interesting insights and perspective rips open a tear in space and time in his life for all to see hear feel touch and taste.

Welcome to my heart journey...

It has no beginning middle or end
(as all of our evolutionary experience is never ending)
Rather this is an open door to the raw rusted sparse landscape that is my stream of consciousness.

This journey follows what might be a timeline of a new relationship and the plethora of happenings that transpire in between.

For your reading pleasure the good bad and ugly.

Here is my heart on these pages stripped bare.

CONTENTS

ACKNOWLEDGMENTS

**"This is an emotional journey
so strap in and hold on"**

Welcome to my heart journey ...

It has no beginning, middle or end (as all of our evolutionary
experiences are never ending)
Rather this is an open door to the raw rusted sparse
landscape that is my stream of consciousness.

This journey follows what might be a timeline
of a new relationship and the plethora of
Happenings that transpire in-between.

For your reading pleasure the good the bad
and the ugly. Here is my heart on these pages
stripped bare.

"he took us on a whirlwind of emotions"
-Austin Macauley

1

FIRST PHASE OF THE RELATIONSHIP (CHEMISTRY)

LIGHTNING STRIKES

A quiet baron wasteland was my heart

Desolate and unused it was an engine that was never supposed to re-start.

Connections came and went

For months it went on like this

Too much time was lost and spent

Many knocked but it was never recognized as intent

To a heart that flat-lined too much time had passed

My mind and heart believed there was nothing anymore that was built to last

The way we met was so unconventional

We had mad chemistry unintentional

You initially walked away and wrote me off as just a friend

That was after the fact to your will I would not bend

I tried to stay away I was better off alone

But I was hurting and vulnerable my heart was a stone

I couldn't resist you I don't deny I was so intrigued

You consumed me so we would chat till I was fatigued

I would fantasize about you all the time

I wanted to touch you I knew it would be sublime

Our friendship has grown now we almost had a kiss

This chemistry electric -A chance to see you I cannot miss

I couldn't contain myself, my heart always racing around you it's true

The next time we met I leaned in and I kissed you...

You ignited something inside that had no spark

A flame now exists where before there was just dark

LOVERS LETTER UNWRITTEN

Manifesting moments

Not yet happened
Not yet enjoyed
Not yet realised

Caringly contemplated in many realities already

In many universes
Completed in our minds
Pleasures

Before during and after

Missing moments weve never had.

THE MEETING PLACE

We have a special place
A place we can go

This is where I meet you now
This is where my intent for you I show

I'm apprehensive and nervous
Just to see you I sneak out of work

Always the same excitement before seeing you
My boss must think I am a total jerk

Before a reason to look forward to work I had not
Our little piece of heaven our little coffee spot

That was always the best part of my long working day
I think about it all the time now
It was the one thing that kept me sane and okay

Any reason to see you I would find or create
My feelings strong now I cannot imitate

What's happening I can no longer control
Attraction heavy and lusty thoughts now prevail
Trying to control this is definitely going to fail

The smell of slow brewed coffee
transports me to a different time
It links my heart to yours somehow
It's into yours I want to unlock and climb

You're holding my hand now there is no race
We have all the time in the world it seems
To discover many anew meeting place

A SECOND IN TIME

I lock eyes with her

A surge of electricity rips through my body

I lock eyes with her

Organized chaos of intentions fall
Lying scattered on the floor of my mind
Like moaning drug addicts in
Withdrawal

I lock eyes with her

So raw this moment
Its stripped down to its most naked form
Not all bad...that's a twisted lie...

Mostly bad

I want to ravage her
Be with her
Be inside her

When I lock eyes with her

I want to give into it
But be in control of it at the same time

Is that even possible

I lock eyes with her

Make it possible...

I see sweet release of grinding loins in her eyes...
I see love personified, electrified
I see friendship set on fire

When I lock eyes with her

I see desire giving into lust
And lust giving into desire
All covered in a moment in time

Time spanning milliseconds.
Time spanning years...
A lifetime in your eyes

All in a second
All in her eyes
All when we lock eyes.

I lock eyes with her
Just for a second in time
For her I long

A fleeting smile A second look
And a second in time
gone.

2

SECOND PHASE OF THE RELATIONSHIP (FALLING FOR YOU)

CLICHÉ CHEMISTRY

I look at you intentions filled
I look at you eternal affliction stirs
My breathe heavy with lust
I want you to stare back knowing we must

I stalk you now
Closer I get
You are my prey
Intentions so fierce and clear
You moan softly you know I'm near

You feel me close
Your body quakes
I kiss your neck
Your leg starts to shake

I move in
Smooth and slow
Dominating in presence
You react you feel my flow

My hand on your back
I slide down low
My breathe on your skin
You pant out then in
What's next you know

My body ripped and hard
Against you I press
I whisper my love
Thrusting first tense
You moan and surrender
Second time round
You let me in so tender

I enter you warm and wet
Our bodies and worlds collide
I make your body explode
Over and over love implodes

You finish quickly
I lie by your side spent
I forget where I am
I recall what I just sent

Over and over
In my mind it plays out
What we did
What was said
Our bodies lie sprawled over the bed

All in a second we slip away
The room so quiet now
Sleep deep now I have consumed my prey
My hard deep love (carried you so far)
To a place beyond heaven
(you can't get there by car)

This ocean of love swept you away
Come back soon to me
I always wish you could stay

Always shallow and empty
I feel once she is gone
I can't fill that void
I need you again
Don't make me wait too long

I'll wait for her return
How long I don't know
Always gone without a trace
And I awake with just reality to face

Will I ever learn
Was it a dream was it real?
Alone again and empty I feel.

THE HIDDEN GIFT – CHAPTER 2 (FALLING FOR YOU)

In the quiet recess of my mind

Your love like light embers glow
I go there when I miss you
It is there you I find

Love packaged with baggage
Conditions and terms I've had too much
Your love just pure just simple
Never have I experienced such

I flash forward often to memories
Not yet made
Pictures not yet taken
Trips not yet had

As much as I try these images I cannot erase

They exist for a future that for us waits...
A hurtful past forgotten
With the excitement of this new fate

A road long and loving together I see us walk
Our friendship strong
Our hearts loving and respected
All bound with lots of talk

It's a long winding road
With no maps in sight
Its ok my love don't fret
Even times we walk at night

Again your heart the way will light
And that love we use
To the darkness we fight

And in the end I don't care where I land
As long as I'm with you
All this I can stand

You see as long as the road may be
If I can walk it with you
By your side holding your hand
And you next to me

Then I'm not afraid to take another step
Because I'll have all I need
You see your love is like my gps
My compass – my guiding light

I thought I was ill equipped
But all the time it was right there
In my lap

You see it was your love
Your guiding light, you...are the hidden gift
My map.

3

THIRD PHASE OF THE RELATIONSHIP
(TRYING TO SAVE IT)

HOLD ON

Hold on

When you're staring down
The barrel of circumstance

You can't explain how you feel
To someone you just dying for a chance

Hold on

When life seems to deal you the hard card
And your tired body of emotions
Can't deal with the fisard

Hold on

Hold on

When thinking is a journey of sad solitude
My mind takes me back to our happier time
That now seems so misconstrued

Hold on

When I sit in a crowded room but feel alone
Like a piercing blow unending I don't recognize
The sound – it's just my phone.

Hold on

Is this really happening
Why do I feel so mad about it?
It's not that...I'm just mad at myself
And actually I*m really sad about it

Hold on

All I know is I remember what we have

All the happiness we bring each other
And how we acted makes us not
Recognize one another

All I know is I have to hold on
Because its you I love
And I believe that is true and strong

Hold on

Let this heavy mist leave us now

Let the clouds clear
And the warm sun kiss your face
I love you baby and you I cannot replace

Hold on

All this to you I write
Strange I have not picked up my pen in a while
This sword I usually do battle with
But now it's out of fret not fight

Battle...that's not my style

Hold on

For I'm sorry for the mistakes I've made
I let myself down
Made my better self frown
I was supposed to be your king
But I dropped my crown

Hold on

I know im not perfect but inn trying to do better
Hearing it out loud now sounds deranged
Please see through me into my heart
Because the me in there hasn't changed

Hold on for me to what you know we have
Hold on to me because you cherish what I gave
Hold on and have faith that our good outweighs our bad

Hold on a little longer

So I can embrace your heart...
Hold it in my hands
Kiss it and tell it "I remember you"
Pull you closer to me
But I can't get close enough
I just want to reconnect but it Seems so tough

Hold on a little tighter

I'm waving you down frantically
I still will do everything I can
I hope you see me
I'm standing on my toes
I'm doing the best I can

Hold on please baby

We will get through it together
We knew it wouldn't be easy but
We can do it together

Hold on

I'm sorry for everything
I don't want to be in this sad place
With you anymore
I know youre angry and I'm also sore

Hold on

I'm trying to make it right...
Reach for you ...
Remind you about our precious light

Hold on

This isn't high stakes poker
A game of life a house of cards
But if it was, on you I would bet it all
I'm all in.
...and for you ill fold.

Just to show you that love isn't in the folding on
Who's wrong whose right?

My love for you I prove is the holding on

Hold on

SAD BUT TRUE

Little hurdles came up to us test
I thought it part of relationship growth
I thought what you and I had was the best

I wrote it off to differences I would get to know
And as time went on your love for me you would eventually
really show

Sometimes I would feel so connected so close
It was like telepathy was our language
But after connecting you would just ghost

I thought I knew what to expect with you
As per what was said and agreed
The truth was that I picked up something else
You were pulling back and needed to be freed

I never felt like I could get really close at all
It was you stopping our progress yourself
Getting close to me you were trying to stall

I could never understand why what you said
And did weren't perfectly aligned
I should have been more careful then
The facts of the situation to myself I should have resigned

But when you're in love you just jump
You just free fall
Because you're fearless and brave
Love makes you feel tall

Your boundaries were never truly defined
And always changing grey and unclear
I realise now that your thoughts and decisions
Were mostly driven by fear

You didn't know where to stand
And if you jumped with me
You didn't know where you might land

All this I gave time for – I understood
The mistake was relying on your word
And believing you would

Jump like I did
No parachute no pressure
I'm pretty sure this is safe
I don't remember this being so scary
Maybe I need a refresher

Can I get some assurance?
Can you give me a guarantee?
I'm taking all the risks here
I could lose my life I could lose myself

The highs of love are supposed to be without measure
The highs of love we are not supposed to bury but treasure

But that doesn't work if you're in it alone
Sometimes I thought the girl I met
Was replaced with a clone

You're just present but not there
A blank space where your opinion was
A little gap where there used to be care

I'm sure she trusts me
I'm sure she'll come around
You'll see she will stand with me
You'll see love with me she's found

But it never got better
It never reached its full potential
But how could it when your focus was
On something else more continental

Now the problem is mine
I'm being too over-zealous
I compromised my standards for you
But I'm the one being jealous

I just wanted you to myself
was that to much to ask
Looks like it was
And loving me to you now has become a task

I'm losing you
The truth is I never had you to start.
You belonged to someone else
You could never give me your heart

Only a part of your soul

You gave me your body instead
Which is worse than death
A path I followed that to nowhere led

A promise of new life I had a taste
But got nothing at all from you
When it came down to it
Just a waste.

4

FOURTH PHASE OF THE RELATIONSHIP (EXISTING IN LIMBO)

FIRST SUNLIGHT - CHAPTER 4 (LIMBO)

I woke up this morning
Confused and anew
Only not new-somewhere lost totally in-between
A place I don't know

This new dark heavy news seems never to leave my side
Like my shadow always there
Like a dirty secret I can't share

I'm trying to get high
Cause I feel so low
Lying to myself constantly
I get all short and snappy
This is bullshit hard work trying pretend I'm happy

Heart ache
Heart break
Heart fake, fuck it's so hard
Head or tails of it to make

Will it always be this way...uphill?
Or will I one day get the release
(Like from medicine or a pill)

DENIED no easy road to take
Though the change I refrain
Numb the pain
Push through
I have to try

Take it one day at a time
So slow at first now – how time starts to fly
Time.
Time heals.
Time heals nothing.

Just a lesson is left there to digest...

I am wiser now, still hurt, don't skirt
Face it
Fess up
Mess up
There is no wrong...

The only wrong is not to try again.

I live to fight another day...

Scars heal
Hearts feel
Strangers connect
And serendipity apparently is real.

5

FIFTH PHASE OF THE RELATIONSHIP
(DEALING WITH THE TRUTH OF IT)

ISN'T IT OBVIOUS

Isn't it obvious to you?
-no it isn't

Yet you walk around like you have all the information
-stop being so unpleasant

I tried to tell you and I asked you to listen
-you won't

Your ex's new girl saw you as a threat
-I wonder why?

When I questioned you about it you said it was just something
you regret...
-that was a Lie!

So you found your ex husbands new girlfriends lingerie in
your childs bag
So now you're thinking ...
- She's the crazy hag

All the while to me you were singing
- That same old song

But you're the one that didn't know what was really going on

She needed to mark her territory
- can't you see that

And doing it the only way she knew how

Why she felt the need to have to do that?
- (not because she is a cow)

She did it because she knew the truth
-you keep trying to hide

It is still your ex-husband you pine for
-you long for him at your side

You are so transparent now
-I can see through you

Your false feelings
-your tainted taste

All the words exiting your mouth
-were just a massive waste

It is fine now I am really content
I dodged a bullet I feel so light

Really what you did to me though wasn't right

But that is the beauty delivered
-when you see things in hindsight

THE BETRAYAL

You seemed too good to be true
You were.

Your mystery and vulnerability drew me in
-For sure.

I believed everything you said
Which was wrong.

When I looked at you I heard angels sing
-It didn't take long.

I fell for you and gave you my best

You lied to yourself and me
That was a test.

You led me down a road that lead to nowhere
And you knew it.

You wanted to have your cake and eat it
So you just said screw it.

Not telling the whole truth is the same as lying.

I should have seen more signs
Inside I did and was dying.

I was in a routine with you
Actually it was a rut.

It serves me right
-I didn't trust my gut.

You act so surprized and hurt like you had done
nothing wrong.

I questioned you about your feelings often
-You always sang the same song.

That was it I was done I did not deserve what I had
been served.

I'll let karma handle you now
-You will get what you deserve.

You held a torch for your ex even after he continually hurt you
outside and in.

I am a better man than he will ever be and you know it.
Your denial was so thick it was a sin.

That's okay though one day you can answer to your maker
What you did to me was a deal-breaker.

I was betrayed and hurt because you could not have
what you desired
-I'm done writing about this is I am over it and
emotionally tired.

THE TRIANGLE

The truth is
I never thought I would be involved
In a relationship like this
Where previous issues were never resolved

You promised it was over and you were getting divorced
I supported you and I gave you the time you needed
I let it run its course

You kept me close and you gave me hope
This game of hangman I didn't realise
Was being played with your rope

You continued to see him
And let him in
Accepting his gifts, gestures and advances
I should have known then nobody would win

Love has a funny way of leaving you blind
No matter what's done to you by love
You just accept and pay it no mind

But that is a dream not reality
And can never work

You're the one that did me wrong
So why do I feel like a fool?
You should feel like the jerk

I am now forced to question
If anything with you was real?

It was pretty real to me
And what is still real
Is this pain I now feel

That's what you get

When you tangle with the three sharp sides

Someone will get hurt
And in the end
There is no one there in which to confide

I realised you must be quite lost
Not knowing if a push Is a pull
Trying to find yourself constantly
That is enough to make anyone ill

You are a very confused person
And didn't know how with any of it to deal
But pushing it down to not deal with
Is the best way time from yourself to steal

The problem is you stole time from me too
Time I will never get back
Time I could have been spending with someone else
A person totally committed and basically less false

This triangle spun me round
Shook me and spat me out
I am all for what does not kill you
Making you stronger
But this was not quite that
My conclusion is to trust in love no longer

So thank you for that
I forgive you and hope you find peace
I leave you with some advice
The girl continually played by her ex husband
Never finds true release

6

SIXTH PHASE OF THE RELATIONSHIP
(NOT DEALING WITH THE TRUTH OF IT)

MEDICATION

Cold and white
In my palm it lays
I'm frozen in perspiration
I stare it down almost in desperation

The weight of my world's problems
All of it so continuous

Could this finally end the night?

This hard pill to swallow
Leave me in my disappointment to wallow
Frustrated by myself Isolated not by choice
I screamed for help but had no voice

It is hard to believe that this is really the hand life has dealt
When all you needed was a sort place to fall
And someone who understood you when you couldn't be tall

Some person who felt what you felt
Could feel what you feel
Could show you the way out of this dense wasteland
of pollution
Only to find out there was no solution.
Somebody to sit beside me while I kneel.

Constant reminders crop up in plain sight
Before these mundane things I took for granted
Normal objects I now stand staring through
My mind lost, off somewhere in past smiles...
So many memories in my mind they que
They seem to go on for miles

Remember that it is not the be all, the end all
And everything that life has to offer you forever.
It is not a life sentence.
This state is temporary.
Even though it feels like it will leave me never.

Once you have learned what you need to
And grown in the way you have to
Your heart will release you... of it all.

Break the chains you couldn't negotiate
Rip you from this dark lonely place you hate
No questions only answers it now gives
Sublime understanding now
Allows evolution from your old self to shed

The feelings of sadness and heartbreak
Were simply a map to which it to you lends
What requirements of your new self
Could not to your old self send.

And the bitter sweet truth
That is left was all that pain
Actually helped you to grow
And was finally a means to a much greater end.

THE ESCAPE

I need to escape

Get away
I am trying to forget my past
Trying to last days flash by so fast
My life is better now
What you reap you sow

But sense of it I still often try to make

Move on outrun
Trying to have fun
Trying to be normal
For sanity sake

In the mornings I wake up
And I put on my smile
Like an item of clothing
It's a lie my smile is fake

It looks normal and bland
I'm not buying it
But to you my smile I'm trying to sell
I walk around angry
I feel like I'm in hell

I hope you don't see
It's a lie I'm covering up
I feel so aware
Don't look at me

Should you be here still?
Visiting me in my thoughts
You come to me so often
But I never get my fill

Like you call for me
I can hear it clearly
Trying to revisit it isn't uphill

But entertaining it is hollow reward
Like a soldier trying to reach enemy lines
Can't I just fall on my sword?

I see you as of old
In my mind it feels real
It's like you are waiting for me to call you
It's your embrace I can't wait to feel

All I have to do is call you
We'll get back together you'll see
Can't we just run away?
That's a plan together we'll flee

I hate that I still think back
To a better time we had
It was so long ago now
Like the 80's it was a lad

I miss us and miss you
And wonder about our alternate endings
Could it have been different?
In my thoughts
It's still love to you I'm sending

I don't miss the fights
We had more than a few
You made me insecure
You weren't over him its true

You don't deserve my thoughts nor my time
So why do I find you here
Clinging on to me
Hoping for happiness
This isn't reality I fear

I thought I was over you
I thought I was moving on
I look everywhere I see you
I hear you in a random song

Is this normal or is this a sign
Will it always be this way?
Never able to escape
For you I always pine

The good the bad
The ugly the unkind
It like the chapters of a story book
The end of which I cannot find

All I can do is hold on tight
And wait for it to pass
The memory of you
To get over it I need to take a class

You always demanded your own pace
You actually gave very little
You saved a special place for him
And that I have to face

And he threw it back at you
And you loved him still!
That I will never forgive or understand
What's wrong with you?
You must be ill.

Release me I beg
I want to escape from this place
Down a long bottomless pit I'll fall
In reality love and hope don't exist for me now
I don't believe in those things at all

It changed me
Being hurt by you
And I cannot go back

I hope you are happy now
This is what you wanted
Was this your plan of attack?

I'll keep my heart under lock and key
This whole love thing
I don't get it I obviously don't see
I don't think I have the knack

My feelings spilled out
I've been writing for a while
I thought I was done with this

I'll just add it to the pile.

I WAS JUST WONDERING

I wonder sometimes what you are doing
-where you are?

Do you still think about me
-are you near or far?

Do you still work at the same place
-or have things changed in your career race?

Do you think about me when you're blue
-do you relive our memories once you've had a few?

Who do you allow now into your space
-is it just anyone now?

Because you're lost and your feelings you don't know how
to face?

Are you looking for answers you cannot find
-do you walk around pretending when you're actually
ignorant and blind?

Do you search for something which you eludes?
-you know if you found it all these mixed up feelings you
could conclude

Who me?
-I'm fine I don't experience any of the above

It was only out of curiosity I asked...
-not out of love.

Is it okay to sometimes admit you feel weak?

I wonder about you
-do we need closure to speak?

I don't have the answers
I don't know the way

I have to just accept that now

I have to just take it day by day.

ALL I CAN DO

I can try to explain
The best day of my life

I can try explain
How a gift from
God Took away my strife

I can try explain
How much for you I love and care

I can try explain
Why I'm so far away
And life isn't fair

I can try explain
That I do everything
With you in mind

I can try explain
That you are dads
One of a kind

I can try to explain
That you make me a better man

I can try explain
That Im your biggest fan

I cannot try explain
That there is a hole in my heart

And that to me you are a work of art

All I can do is try to put into words
How much I miss and love you
And being away from you is rough

But the words...the words aren't enough...

All I can do is write the ode to you and hope

One day when you're old enough to comprehend

That it's just dad with all his love for you he was trying to send.

7

SEVENTH PHASE OF THE RELATIONSHIP (RE-ALIGNING ONE'S PRIORITIES)

THE PARASITE

What do I do with this pain...

I sit with it attached to me
Not by choice
From it I try always detach
My energy from me it drains

I walk I try to run
I eat I try to drink and this pain
I think I will smother

I carry it like shame
An open wound
A nerve exposed
This pain I try to cover

Feelings?
They come up and I reflect
They surface and visit and I deflect
I push them down deep
Their safer there like a treasure
To protect

Down deep down
Down – 1
Down – 2
Down – 10

To The toilet bowl
I cling with urgency
I've just got a broken heart
No emergency.

It comes up again and again
This must be the therapy I need?
That is a lot of alcohol I think
Am i planting a bad seed

While my body I try restrain
To The toilet bowl cold hard I'm attached

The universe's therapy cruel and continuous delivered
A matted web of thoughts swirl non-stop I'm dizzy
My breathing all the while I'm trying to regain

Is this how I release the pain?
All I want to do is shout, kick and fight
I'm back in bed how did I get here
Self-pity begins again and too the numbness
I beg for time to hurry all I want is the night

I look around and the only people left in my life
Are trying to help me
But their judgments just bring me strife
My self-judgements way worse
On this insignificant life

The words they speak intended to nurture
Nothing u say works
Your lips shut I want to suture

Every attempt to claw back something of a life
Just brings a new problem – a new angle
A deeper problem brand new revealed
More strife.

My old friend calls to me
And you stare through an empty glass
Back in this familiar place I think
"Did I finish that drink already – God that was fast."

I wake up on the floor at last
Lock me away
Take me to a place nobody knows
I need a doctor
A clean slate

It's that answer I need and seek
If I don't find it soon
My new residence
A dirty cell mate

You have taken everything from me
I have nothing left of myself
An empty shell I stare at
Is not the me I once knew.

Just your voice in my head I hear
You keep saying "cmon lets go have a few"
SHUT UP! Just.leave.me.alone.
I look up I'm alone and even the voice is just gone.

Someone with their arm around me
Whispers "daddy can you get up?"
Is this my son? When did he grow up...

I am sorry my son for all I put you through
You see this parasite called alcohol
Took daddy for an hour or two

But I am back and better
I promise you'll see...
I'll do right by you
I'll make it right

That nasty parasite I realise
Was not the alcohol that stole
Me, my life, my time with you as a whole

The real thief
The actual parasite here was me.
The selfless actions of a broken heart
Robbed me of you
And now finally I can start

To love you and get to know you
To discover you and grow
With you and spend time
And show you the things a man's supposed to know

I'm sorry I'll do better
You deserve so much more
And you simply say "its fine daddy I love you"
It was always you...
- You're my cure.

8

EIGHTH PHASE
(BOOMERANG) – WHEN YOU THINK YOU OVER
SOMEONE YOU LOVE AND YOU SEE THEM AGAIN

HELLO STRANGER

You walked past me in the street today
It stopped me cold
I stood there a while
Not knowing what to say

And a chapter of my past was instantly retold...

It already must have been more than 2 years
I don't want to really remember
There was a lot I still missed
I don't miss the fights, lies and tears

Nothing left of that person anymore.

You are just a complete stranger now
When I think about how intimate we once were
There is still a dark sharp sting I try not to allow

I was forced to look at this once sacred place

Standing so physically close for a second
Internal proximity usually shared
By comparison was now
Worlds apart and mostly impaired

Sad and shocking when I think it through
How did we get here again?
Oh I remember it was you.

It's just a part of life I suppose?
Just one more thing I will never understand
Just one more thing
I need to accept and compose

Consistently I feel I've made internal progress
Only for the universe to set me back
I feel like all I did is just regress

Am I making headway at all?
Why do I feel like I've been knocked down.
Like after a fall

The truth is I know the answers
To the questions – I admit
I just don't like the answers
Because none of them seem to fit

The pieces I slowly pick up and put back
One by one I try make them click and make sense
I try pretend I'm intact and there's nothing I lack

But the only resolution

That is actually left are the facts
And those are cold and stark
The thought of all of it
Always makes me feel so dark

For now all I can do is breathe
Here in this state I stand for so long
I waited there frozen
Until your presence and aura was gone

I didn't know what to do next
So I continued to walk
All I could do was shake my head
And to myself continue to talk

I won't allow myself
The pleasure this time
Of replaying what could have been
And be pulled down emotionally
For a future never actually seen

Instead I leave you with silent numbness
And mumble to myself

Hello stranger
And a sad goodbye
The truth of it is
What I wanted with you
Was always all a lie

I let go of it now
As I watch you walk away...

Just another person
Of another lifetime
Of another day.

9

NINETH PHASE (CHOOSING HOPE)

THE PURSUIT
(THERE IS ALWAYS HOPE)

Maybe just maybe you long for a new life
we cannot see much without hope
It is hard to broaden arisens with a narrow scope

I try to practice positive thoughts
But when inclined to be positive
The results get more negative
It is not like I'm not trying I am!

For now I look for advice
I follow the crowd
I try hide my pain
My thoughts they feel so loud

I look around for love
Maybe someone else can give me hope
Alone though I remain
I start to carry this load with aggravated distain

The gravity of this pursuit
It visits me when my thoughts take time off
That is more often than not
I feel overwhelmed and destitute

I trudge on I must try
Push on push through
Break the chains I chose to carry
I feel like this this pain inside
I'm about to marry

My soul feels kicked punched and stomped on
This is a heavy weight bout
When it is easier to give in
Give up
Surrender to doubt

When all I need is some inspiration
I look left I look right
And all people give me is bland information
Is there nothing I can use?

Know this the multiverse is working for you
Have some faith and let it
Don't refuse
Your emotions and fear cloud your vision
But this flickering little bit of light you must not lose

Load the gun
Tighten the noose
You pull the trigger
Nobody will miss me anyway
I figure

In one moment right before the end
Your situation can change
You feel the earth move
You gasp for air
And you feel it there

Like it's the first time
You have been allowed to breathe
And the relief is clear
Remove the noose now
From your neck

Step down off the guillotine
Drop the blade
The universe does care about me
Don't let this feeling fade

What is this old returning friend
So full of light
by some force to me being led
That there is hope
It was inside you! – Not being fed

You were feeding doubt
And giving up when all you
Wanted to do was stay in bed

Your perception now different
Even though your circumstances
Haven't changed that much

So what is it then that feels so different
So restored and so new
Fear has left me now
I am released from its clutch

I only see answers and opportunity
I am thankful and full
Hope warm and tender
Surrounds me now

Its embrace imparts me with much ease

I am bursting now
I can see joy
My blurry eyes wet with
Involuntary release

All I needed was to feed hope
In the end I realised this simple truth
And the by-product of hope...
Was inner peace.

10
TENTH PHASE (LESSONS IN HINDSIGHT)

THE LESSON

Life is a priveledged lesson
It is up to us to deal with
And not pick a side good or bad

It is not our job to understand it
But to find peace in it and acceptance
Though it may make us sad

And therein lies the growth and development
That which we resist with all our being...
That imprisons our emotions
Is the same thing required to do all our freeing

So have faith
Be patient and invest in yourself
Because at the end
All your experience will directly relate
To your emotional wealth

And this once crazy world
That we viewed as our hungry enemy
Will reveal all its secrets

And we will learn
That it was not done
To make us feel like fools

But rather to equip us with the one
Thing we always lacked

The tools.
Lesson learnt.

THE PARK BENCH

I sit here on this park bench alone
I write down my thoughts
Here I'm the king on my throne

Pulled the wool over my eyes
You made me feel like a fool
But hey that's ok
I sit here and in solitude I'll rule

I want to reboot
Start again
Control alt delete
A new page a new mantra
It's with myself now I compete

I realise more and more
I made the right call
To stand by my standards
And not just for anything to accept or fall

I take into my hands
My own destiny
My own fate
I see now with no standards
Your opinions carried no weight

I'm in control and empowered
And I am chasing my dreams
No one can stop me now
Not even you anymore it seems

So I may sit here alone
On this park bench I'm fine
But it is by choice I'm here alone
And that choice was mine

I have grown and evolved
Without that pain I would not be here
My eyes have been opened there is nothing to fear

I wield my sword and my shield
Not with weapons I fight
With words I do battle
With words I show my might

So as I finish
Another masterpiece I conclude
That the core of me is still alive
And it is forward in motion I now need to strive

I'm at peace as I write
The pen mightier than the sword
I look up and say thank you
I am blessed and finally recognize it Thank you lord

THE DAMAGED JOURNEY

Let it all go
Just let it drift away

Don't let it show
The injury.

Be strong
They don't know you
They don't know your damage.

You don't have to carry it anymore
You don't have to protect this pain
You don't have to nurture it to feel sane

Just let the gravity of it go.
Open the doors and set it free

A paralysed moment
A smack of relief
A concuss realisation

Birds flight free
See them swarm
See them

Watch them
Transport escourt that bad energy
They fly away slow and steady beyond the sea

Ushered away
Smothered less someday
Weightless now
Nothing needed of words to say

All that exists now is this tranquil place
I look around and its familiar

This cage
These walls
This broke unhinged door

Its metal
Its wood
Its misunderstood
Its free

Its finished now its familiar

Its me.

THE DANCE

No more hiding

Life is not painless
Allow the buried warmth to rise
Freeze the setting sun

To awaken and peak
Frosted breath into that dark place
You refuse to acknowledge

That moment encased in glass
That screams fragile
That you refuse to break

Break it
Smash it open
Tear into that rough coarseness

Pull apart the common sense
You have been using as your narrative
For only through daring death

Is blind rebirth relinquished
Only then can pain and pleasure truly be measured
Only then can you receive the gift of value

All moments
All relevant
All inclusive
All different but part of the same

Suffering and joy dance long into the night

The past
Quick glances down a dark corridor
All those feels mute now.

I muted them
So now only parts of pictures seem to
Seep through.

Leave the past in the past they say
BUT these pictures of the past
Now faded and jaded are slowly
Becoming overdeveloped

Someone opened the door to that red room
Someone interrupted the developing wounds.
Someone distracts me now from revisiting those
tortured places.

The murmuring memories
That underwhelmed understanding
Like a new guest eagerly awaiting a hotel room

You stand there naive
Like a bouquet of all my favourite unanswered questions
Enticing...intriguing.

You stand filling up the doorway.
You hold my attention so well
So intensely — I forget the past ever existed
For a moment

My heart now smiling turns to see
Where all the light is being pulled to.
Like a vacuum you pull everything in

You.
Still standing there unknowingly
Shining and sparkling like fresh wet grass.

You make me understand that the past is not purgatory.
The past is the evidence of fixed pieces which now fill all that
I lost.

Serenity of ones tired emotions
The post cursor to serendipity.

The penny on the floor...
That realization unpaused
My life song awakened

I get it now
I finally understand.

THE CORRUPT RECKONING

Boundaries clear
Rules set
Discussions agreed
Never forget

You walk the line
Most times you blur it
Line in the sand
Pretend I drew it

You look me in the eye
Like its fine

The boat now rocked
The waves now shocked
The ripples created
The message inundated

The balance you forced
The zen you lost
Your point you dotted
Your T you crossed

The truth
You tip toe around it
No code
The lies you lay with

A version you self-told

Our government
A zero soul machine
And the result

Our citizens out sold.

THE SHADOW

Im trying to lose it
I try to shake it off
This growing attachment, this uninvited guest
It reminds me of prison

The visiting hours do not apply here
Breaking and entering as you please
A felony just accepted as one of life's gifts

Like on my birthday
Except it isn't.
I don't want this thing you call a gift.
I don't want something that takes from me all I have some days
And leaves me with nothing most days

I dream of the sun
A place less dark
The sun it comes out warm and inviting
Soothing that cold place
Melting that icy plane

The drip drip and melting melancholy
Brings hope of a better time
But the truth is right there again
Hidden but also in plain sight

Like a shadow that does not belong to me
I check once, I turn and check again
Just to make sure its mine and is attached to me

I don't get to enjoy the sun, not even a little
Shallow atonement in memories is all I now get
I used to curse the clouds
I don't do that anymore

Now, I don't mind the grey
That place between black and white
I have discovered it is the only time I now get to myself that
Doesn't cost so much

These are the prices you make me pay
These memories of you
Before you.

THE STAND OUT

Red lips offset blue eyes

She likes long looks – locked in

Feels like a moment

Her gaze goes on ...

For what feels like a mile

For milliseconds

Frozen in my mind

A Millenia in my heart

SKYDANCING

You there...Of earth

And of other Earth...

The gifts to see

The curse you cant

Window watcher

Opener

And message carrier.

You peer through windows to another plane...

To catch a message not always meant for you.

Not always meant for your eyes but meant always for hearts

And souls.

Souls who have hearts and souls who don't.

Traffic in the skies.

THE INNER CALL

That voice inside calls to you
If you listen you can...

Listen to the wind whisper
Knock on the moon
Tap on the stars

Call to the morning sky
Taste that orange hue of dusk

Feel the echoing of memories call from the burnt desert
Sit and bathe in the healing waters of its oasis

Shake of the dust
This is what we all must do

To heal.

VERSES OF SELF

Under the covers
Are the pages of me
They exist in my consciousness

They define my personal reality

I don't judge books on covers anymore
They are my dreams
My hopes
These pages warmly wrap my essence

And safely seduce me
Into sharing chapters of my journey

Letting go easing off into a place where all the dreams happen
The real standard to judge
Is the simple successful escape of the daily dogma

To question it all
Until release
Until the exhale is final

RECOVERY

Walking wounded
With limp limbs I lambaste in the mess I call my life
These bandages bound to me look like
A shell of normalcy

I should go so I don't stay
I let you into my heart only to have you walk away
It was a head on collision
Accidental but now

Nothing can fill up this space
These cracks in my haemorrhaging heart
After the wreckage they seep and weep

No operation was done
No therapy
No balm
No soothing self-discovery

My hearts written off
With no insurances there is no claim
To recover what I lost

YOU GET WHAT YOU GIVE

Life is good to the good

It lends from one your very own actions...

It smiles on you when you have something to smile about

Simply smile and wait for the warmth of her nature to start the nurture.

Trust her
She is smiling back.

THE GIRL WITH THE SHACKLED HEART

She sits in the dark room
Pondering if she will ever be free
She just wants to feel

She remembers it
She remembers what it is like
But like a damp ember

Trying to ignite it again is futile

Will she ever feel anything again
She reaches for connection
But these prison bars tighten their grip

Past hurt
Past pain
Past lessons
These are her chains

Learned not learned and unlearned

All stand around her
Like walls of a tower
The more she reaches
The more they tighten

She doesn't remember what its like to feel anymore

Numb darkness is her shackled new state
Because taking a leap of faith is something in which she
refused to participate

Breaking the shackles will require immense strength
But sitting In this place she doesn't deserve
Nor belong

Will take from her even more

There is a choice to be made here
We get to choose our kind of pain
But the cost of that pain is the biggest choice of all

UNRIPENED

Creative ideas
Dying on the vine Drip.
Sway.
Dropping off
Like over heavy dead fruit
Ripening to the truth.

They lay torn open staining the ground
The question and answer is in front of us
It plays out in muffled cries
Anguished victims buffed by an unstoppable system

The rise of a new reality has an ugly cost
Don't look away
Don't pretend not to see all in pain around you

If you want a new world first remember what you
Will be forced to give up.

Now.
Yes only now you may cry
Weep, for as a new reality breaches the horizon
With it waning dreams set

Dreams of a better time
Close their eyes
Weep for dreams we gave up on.

Dreams they stole.

THE WORTHLESS WORD

The worthless word
Your value now gained
When you promised on your word

When you delivered it in your eyes I saw strain

You birthed your words and behind it
Your stamp with your values you hid

The pregnant pause after the fact
The proven words none of them in tact

To only raise suspicion
To only cover your truth

So your value now fallen
So your worth now defeated

Before you knew it
Before all the drama

I knew it and saw it
Now we wait

For karma.

THE LIFEBOAT

At every turn
A city of sinners and truthful liars
They believe their own tales

I spit on falseness
In my mind justice is served to them but
The unfair truth is in reality
That they all bask in the false truth of their own Glory

Life of titantic proportions
Its passengers blinded by 1st class privilege
And a promise of wealth and upper levels
Beg to be anything but
Promising to not be mundane

Escape what it offers
Help me escape this place
The ignorant acceptance
Floating away now with full knowledge
Knowing now what the acceptable entails

My awakening
My fiery rebirth
The shroud of sheep following sheep now a distant echo
That life left to looters of classes

The big metal machine
With it no engine no compass
No map I can follow
Just fear beside me
Doubt around me
But hope once dead now rising inside me

Hope is enough to deliver me
I faithfully give up all allegiance
Her majesties floating tank
And with it my proposed dream
Which drowned a long time ago

A find.
a secret.
a lifeboat.
I climb into the transport

This vessel of new life?

I wonder to myself where and what it promises
Instead I give in. I get in.
I realise escape means giving up steering anywhere
Surrender to the currents

Surrender the illusion of control
To take me where only a leap of faith can show me

The further I drift away from the mothers breast the more I see
The clarity being fed to me as if with each ticking meter
Once mysterious clues are revealed as new
Pieces to my now new ever growing map

Light up small cervices to invade dark places
To find whats new
To discover versions not yet discovered
I had to put all my faith into giving up control

And let this little life boat decide to show me

The truth.
The way.
The flow.

The universe always loved me
I just had to let it.

IN THE REFLECTION

In the reflection
I stare I stop
Dulled out, drained of colour
A little worse for wear

When I reflect staring there
On a lifetime of hurt
What seems like so many chapters now
Just looks like a page

The answers slowly reveal themselves
Even if I do not like the answers I now know
That I, yes me, I have the ending to write
The ending I was always going to choose alone

So staring for a second I look deeper
I see a little light in the micro chasms of eyes
Blinded by life before we're now waking up
They shake themselves off and slowly let go
Of the self-told lies

And there in that plethora of moments
I managed a wry smile
Understanding how far I had come

Meters and miles
Months without moments finally

In the reflection
I realise – is where all the blessings showed me
All I needed to see.

LOST TRANSLATION

A heart so full
Emotions swollen burst and exhale
At the exhausted seams

Stretching and reaching for closure

Some undeniable understanding that would or possibly
Even could explain this pain

Like a lost child in a busy mall
That cold reality's sudden chill
Just gone.

The words are lost to you.

The empty idea of what needed to be set free
Now pushed down
Forced back down and put to sleep

Like a naughty child past its bedtime

The overwhelming feeling
Yes another one
That an opportunity was just lost
The sad sensation of a last didge attempt

I am misunderstood once more.

Let the grieving begin anew
What I try to save I break.
Again.

NOSTALGIC NAPALM

I read our old conversations

Conversations of you
When I miss it...you...us.
Its like your standing right there
But you're not.

Its like a bridge I build in my mind
It's all access
Always open
It's my direct connection to you

I visit it often
Im sort of a big deal around here
Ive got my VIP stamp
But the truth is I'm not
Important.

It's a bridge between our memories
And I get to go there
To that sacred place To visit you
But only when I need you.

You couldn't. wouldn't
But I can and do.

The truth is
I go there often now
I find myself lost
Lost in the layers of you
A maze of memories

I turn its pages
I watch our love over and over
In stages
Waves of episodes
Hooked like my favourite series

One, two
Ten, twelve.

I know the endings
All of them.
And they are great really they are

But there is something so magical
About our beginnings
Moments
Moments of little waves which
I know would eventually
Bring the tsunami

It makes me weak
Still.
When the earth shook that day
It sucked in the ocean
Like to breathe us in.
We did not image what was coming...
Beautiful demolition

When im around you
Its like flame playing with gasoline
Tietering catastrophe
I know all it takes is

One touch
One text

The weakness still with me
Thoughts of it gives me fireflies
Like but butterflies
But lit up – ignited for all to see
Burning bright for a while – fleeting.

Promises to remember it all
And keep it alive I cannot keep anymore
I pretend its romantic
But it's not anymore

Then crashing realisation comes
This is the worst of it
My best part

I see it
Across eons
Through light years
Spanning dimensions
We always fit

You were made for me.
But it never ends well.
Not once.
Not ever.

SHE DOESN'T KNOW

She doesn't know she even has a light.

I see something in her
Something she doesn't know she has

I see it in her smile.
Not the small ones.
The big ones.

She has that naive curiosity
I see it in her eyes
Wrapped in childlike innocence

Dashed with a little bit of fun
A little bit of naughtiness.
It's in a glance

It lights up the room.
The whole room.
Everything.

She doesn't know it was dark before she walked in.
She looks around and sees light too.
But she thinks its everyone else's light that is also shining.
Hers is the only light I see.

Its warmth makes me brave enough to shine mine.
Even though my world has been dark for so long now...
Her light makes me believe in mine.

All I ask is nothing... Nothing big.

Just leave your light on For me.

ANYMORE

She knew the words to my favourite song

The one we always sang together in the car
Those colourful car trips back to your house changed.

I never noticed at first because I was doing my best to stay
in key.

I look over now and your not even singing anymore.
Your mouth was muted.

You don't know my words anymore.

And in that moment is when it dawned on me.
That slow sinking realization.

Your mouth wasn't the only part of you that was closed to
me anymore.

I don't sing anymore.

I don't sing at all.
Anymore.

SO THERE IT IS

My journey thus far
Just like scattered shards the broken pieces of me are just that
Broken.

And that's okay.

But not how I thought and while the ongoing work
and operation
Continues to recover those damaged arteries this heart
continues to beat!

My realization taken from all this is that a failed heart bypass
Was a necessary event

For all my trying to fix
For all my good doings
For all my lessons

I learned that we are all already
The latent potential and answer
To everything we lack
To everything we need

Negative things happen for us to shape and mould us into
a better
Stronger version of ourselves.

And that is priceless and for that I am eternally grateful.

So this is where I sign off for now

I hope this resonated or birthed fully a new perspective
for you.

If it has even for one of you, if even on of these pieces of my
breaking heart made
Sense then my mission reached a meaningful oasis.

Thank you for reading my most personal and inner emotional ramblings

Let us toast to the beauty and catharsis that is poetry and that is life!

With respect and love thank you
Bruce Martin

Made in the USA
Columbia, SC
21 November 2022

71182196R00046